C00 48851303

Between then
eight children,
one current husband and a stack
accolades. Difficulties getting pre
abortions, caesarians, post-natal
and single parent issues have all featured in their lives and are
reproduced in this collection. Meeting at poetry nights in the
South West Hannah and Thommie discovered each other in a
world that so often shies away from talking about the realities
of motherhood and found a partner with whom to share all their
mothering joys and woes.

Both proud feminists, Thommie and Hannah have previous
collections published by Burning Eye – *My Stepmother Tried to
Kill Me* and *Laid Bare*. They perform individually and together
across the country and hope that this collection opens some
dialogues that have previously been reserved for secret rooms.

WITHDRAWN

MILKED

Thommie Gillow
Hannah Teasdale

Burning Eye

EDINBURGH LIBRARIES	
C0048851302	
Bertrams	22/02/2019
	£9.99
CE	HQ759

BurningEyeBooks
Never Knowingly
Mainstream

Copyright © 2018 Thommie Gillow and Hannah Teasdale

The author asserts the moral right under the Copyright, Designs and Patents Act 1988 to be identified as the author of this work.

All rights reserved. No part of this publication may be reproduced, stored in a retrieval system, or transmitted, in any form or by any means without the prior written consent of the author, nor be otherwise circulated in any form of binding or cover other than that in which it is published and without a similar condition being imposed on the subsequent purchaser.

This edition published by Burning Eye Books 2018

www.burningeye.co.uk

@burningeyebooks

Burning Eye Books
15 West Hill, Portishead, BS20 6LG

ISBN 978-1-911570-27-1

Printed & bound by ImprintDigital.com, UK

MILKED

"'Milked' is a collection of poetry you may not want to read, but you must. They are brutal, shocking but tender poems of women too angry and frightened to follow the script about motherhood that friends, family, medical professionals, strangers try to foist upon them. With expert use of form, judicious choice of detail and a felicitous use of language, as remarkable as their honesty, Teasdale and Gillow show you their scars, their blood-soaked knickers, their semen-stained sheets, the times they felt nothing, or worse than nothing, for their babies, the times they forgot to put their children first. This is the abattoir called human reproduction in all its ugly, shameful, unspeakable wonderfulness."

Melanie Branton – Poet

"Thommie and Hannah have succeeded in birthing the entirety of their experience as parents in a collection that offers a genuine, witty and beautiful instruction manual for life."

Rebecca Tantony – Poet and Bath Spa Lecturer

"For some of us, motherhood is a succession of sunny days leaving a trail of happy memories. These poems speak to all mums, though - the ones who have problems conceiving, the ones who have problems believing this is actually how it is; the ones who are relieved when finally their children grow up, somehow, to be wonderful human beings. Some of the poems are raw with pain; others glow with love. If you want to know - and feel - all sides of motherhood, read this book."

Brenda Read-Brown - Gloucester Poet Laureate

"This powerful collection of high quality poetry provides a beauty of language and elegance of wit that pervades through even the darkest and most difficult experiences. With its resplendent imagery a patchwork of ink, blood, tears and hardships, this collaboration exemplifies the modern feminist, the guilty feminist, and the celebration of the rhetoric surrounding motherhood. By effectively pinpointing the uncomfortable truths and the overlooked miracles of everyday life, 'Milked' is as relatable and necessary for mothers as much as it is educational and thought-provoking for anyone else."

Danny Pandolfi – Raise the Bar

CONTENTS

RED CLOVER

ROSEMARY

RASPBERRY LEAF

RIOJA

For our children:

Oscar, Alfie, Joe,
Billy, Fred, Hope,
Millie and Barnaby

RED CLOVER

TRYING

I want to make love,
to screw like we are
young whippersnappers,
stop,
fuck again,
flip each other over,
slap and tickle and suck.

I want to feel energised
in my nudity,
fling my arms
and legs
in all directions
on your chest,
laugh and laugh and laugh,
come and come and come again
and come
now...
we are older now.

I want to make love,
lie in front of fires,
wiggle your bits,
prod you,
poke you,
open my legs
and my heart
to you.

I want to feel your hands
on my hips
like an urgent
pull in my groin,
not the mutual monthly chore
we smile through.
I want to come and come and come again
but come

now…
we are older now.

We take my temperature.
I want to raise it.

I want to make love,
to pretend we're rabbits
with a thirty-one-day incubation period
and no worries about our age.
I want to prop a pillow
under my hips
just because
I need you
deeper,
harder,
faster.
To hell with gravity.
Fuck gravity.

I want to make love
out of the diary,
not pre-planned,
to run my hands all over
you because you feel good,
you feel good,
not to make you feel
good
thing we have tissues by the bed.

I want to make love and
not be thinking about babies
'cause there's something kind of
creepy in that…
that we make love
but we're thinking about the kids
we want to have.
I want to smear your body in chocolate body paint,
lap it off you

like I'm an over-enthusiastic puppy,
not stress
about the mess
on the sheets.

I want to come at the same time as you,
before you and after you,
then after you again.
You can be smug,
hand me a pint glass after,
say, *Was that four times you came?*
Or five?
I want to not know the answer.

I want to make love tonight.
It's the wrong night.
I want to make love like
it's the wrong night
all night
every night.
I want to make love
and maybe
a baby.

THE TRAP

I do not sleep.
Naked and prone
like a corpse stabbed
through a gap in the spine
where only the heart bleeds out
Muscles twitch in cold sweats
to remind me I am still
awake. Awake still.
Fourteen nights since
in hot forgiveness
you came and death met you
in a copper cage. I wait
for my conscience
to arrive.

FREE

If I would have your baby
we could name her   'Free'.
She'd have your eyes: green,
yet flecked with the darker shade
of mine and framed with a thick
scatter-thrashing   of lashes
to tangle with my abundant hair
and brush the cheekbones
of your flawless olive skin.

She would be the strength in me
and the warmth in you, flesh conceived
in the image of our dream.
Weaknesses: chocolate
and dark-eyed men,
but with unfaltering
self-control and feathered wings
to guide her. She would always be

                                    free,

though she would never
be as others see – you'd teach
her well: to believe in   herself
with curiosity,
more than a reflection   of her peers.
She would always measure up
well, yet never fall foul   of conformity.
She would make huge leaps   of faith.
Naturally, she would be born
to change the world.

PIPE CLEANERS

It's time to clean the pipes
but we are lazy
victims of the middle ages,
a child
and full-time work.
We do not have the necessary
elbow grease it takes.
He says his elbow aches.
I say my jaw does.

We know we have to clean the pipes.
He drank beer at the weekend
and it might affect the flow.
We know
it doesn't have to be good,
so we are half-hearted.
If *perfunctory* weren't already a word
I would coin it for the cleaning of the pipes:
perfunct –
discharged,
discharged funk.

It's time to clean the pipes,
got to get them clear for Saturday,
big night.
I'm trying to be positive
but really we know
neither of us cares.
Can you do it on your own? I say.
I guess. He shrugs.
But we agreed to be partners.

We clean the pipes together.
It is the right thing to do.
I hold him and after
he makes me tea,
we go to bed.

This is what it will be like
with a baby, he says:
teamwork.
At least then, though,
the pipes won't need cleaning
anymore.

COME HOME

I do not care if you cannot make me come.
I bought Ann Summers products to make that happen.
But do I care that you do. You have to.
I do not care if your day's been tough
or if you're suffering with stress, I do not care
if the football's on or your best mate needs you.
Not tonight. My womb needs you.
I do not care if we forget to kiss. Actually, I don't even want to.
Do not bother to take off your socks. Or your coat.
I'll just pull my knickers to one side,
lie on the sofa and open my legs.
Forget the foreplay – that's a pleasure for a different day.

It's day fourteen. And I can feel the eruption
from one ovary. I can feel the squeezing through my tube,
the stretch across my belly like I'm already
three months with child. My nipples hurt and egg-white
discharge soaks my pubes. My temperature is raised
one centigrade and my cervix is so high
I doubt a metre stick could reach it.

Do not turn off your phone. Do not excuse yourself
with a different deadline. We took our vows
and for better and for worse, you will thrust yourself
inside me and make this baby real.
We only get this chance twelve times a year.

ACRONYMS

TBH I can't decide if I hate
or love AF.
She stops me getting
those BFNs that make me want to FML
and then at least I and DH know
it's a no,
it's time to start planning
the next BDs,
but it still makes me ROFC.
(I think I made that one up.
Work it out.)

It's been four months since my last MC,
which BTW was my fifth
after two years of TTC.
I feel like I'm a child again,
back in confession.

I confess:
I wish I didn't know these words
so well.
I wish I didn't feel the need to spend
so much time
on BBC.
That I didn't track my BT or CM
or feel so much pressure to DTD.
TBH I can't decide if I love
or hate wishing.
I just know I can't stop.
KWIM?

PERIODS

My body is playing tricks on me,
dangling my period before me
like Pavlov's carrot,
except it isn't a reward
and it wasn't even Pavlov;
I'm just mixing theories
to keep my mind from
hoping,
planning,
praying
like the last two years have
conditioned me to do.

I wee on a stick.
It is still a stick even if
it isn't Pavlov's.
It feels like a punishment.

PRINTS

When you lift the receiver, you are manic,
yet you know this panic will soon be superseded
by another bout of hollow sadness. Breathlessness
from the masking tape
that binds your lungs,
sticks your uterus to your heart and stops
your eyes from closing
these coming nights.
It will sometime, somehow
find itself undone.

It will peel away, clog your veins. It will fill
your mouth with the inevitable taste of blood.

You don't know when.

In the meantime, you will fill this page
with ink, words that etch like the scars
across your middle. Stains like the prints

inside your knickers
every month.

NEW FRIENDS

Fifty-year-olds,
fifteen-year-olds,
drug takers,
radical anti-procreators,
hysterectomies,
vasectomies,
singles
and people with implants they've no intentions of removing.
These are the folks for me.

Post-menopausal women
who've been there,
done that.
People who drink
too much
and don't want to stop.
People who never have sex
because they're asexual
or too tired
or impotent
or Sheldon from the *Big Bang*
or just have a failing libido
and won't take Viagra.

Ten-year-olds – 'cause they're too young –
and dogs and cats and hamsters
and the woman across the road
who already told me
she's not interested in nappies anymore.
Oprah Winfrey.
Ricky Gervais.
Jennifer Aniston.
These are the folks for me.

I think I'm going to ditch the others.
The ones I already have,
the dangerous ones,

the smilers,
first-timers,
second-time-easys
and accidentallers,
those rhythm method failers who want sympathy.
I think I'm going to ditch
the morning sickness moaners,
the making-a-family-homers,
the hip-separating cabbage-craving groaners.
Just for a bit.
Just 'til it's safe
to answer the phone again,
to go on Facebook.

Fifty-year-olds.
Gateway women.
I need some new friends.

LIFE

Yet another baby has been born,
more photos and happy smiles,
prams and nappy bags popping into work.
My husband takes his lunch break early,
phones me.

It isn't often I hear him choke on his words.

GAMING

He wasn't the one to tell me
or his father, but his younger brother
by a year in a giggle frenzy
of Snapchat history flashed at me
with a combination of envy and fear.

The youth's gospel, judgment-givers
gossip-mongers and virus-spreaders
of present-day. Lives stamped in emojis.
Swollen bellies in different colours.

Sentences of three letters. Someone else's
in-jokes everyone found funny
and nobody opted out of. I bribed him
to tell me, to face me - lose the story

and ride his own reality bareback,
unprotected from the agony. His face
blanked, reminding me of the little boy
who always refused a speaking part
in his primary school Nativity -
he would never follow the script.

I drove them early the next day, both
in the back seat, plugged into phones
to dilute my presence. Then dragged
their misunderstood trainers
to the plastic waiting area where I found

the same seat sixteen years before
with his difficult head wedged
in the wrong place and drank coffee
because it was something to occupy my hands.

Her name was called,
the first time I'd heard it in full.
The first time I'd seen what he had seen
for weeks. She reappeared, stunned
to half her age. I cashed her prescription
whilst they individually updated their story.

LYING

I have lain in a bed of blood and replayed that mating song,
washed myself with tears, cramps on my womb and my heart.
I have mustered words of congratulations from hollow ribs
and smiled like I enjoy the tune the rest of the world is singing.

I have pretended magnanimity is an attribute I possess in
abundance.

I have heard stutters of uncertainty in happy news,
like a tentative John Cage riff from *Ocean of Sound*.
I have lifted myself from my sickbed and carried those
who sing with wariness and choked on their chords.

I have pretended magnanimity is my potion and my cure.

I have watched stomachs swell and visited babies who
surpassed
my own. Passed on clothes I wanted to wear and bought new.
I have lain in a bed of blood and heard that mating song
refrain,
hesitant, worried, apologetically joyful and full of life.

I have pretended I am okay with this.
I lie.

ECTOPIC

My chances are not halved –
they are sure to let me know
that losing a tube reduces fertility, yes,
but doesn't halve it.
Our bodies are amazing –
they say
we adapt.

I learn to make a joke of it –
my one fallopian tube,
it's the left one, I say,
thank goodness,
at least if I do have a baby
he won't be conservative,
we're all a little to the left
in my clan.

In secret I count days with more voracity
than normal.
Our sex life becomes more regimented
than either of us can endure.
I am militant,
unattractive,
impossible to please.

My chances are not halved –
I think perhaps my sanity is.

WHEN SHE SAID (I)

When she said 'Termination' I was just 24
I heard the words
fear
misery
regret
She assured me I was wrong
and that she had no doubts
but I was 24
I knew better
I was not afraid of
single parenthood then
I craved
drama
challenge
stories
I was never pro-life
and it was her body
but we were 24
I knew better

When I repeated the word to her 10
years later
I finally understood
I was unwitting single mum
unplanned
alone
I said doing my best for one
child by refusing
another
I was 34
I said the words
certain
assured
need
she believed me
she knew better

WHEN SHE SAID (II)

At just 24

the words:

Fear
Misery
Regret

She had no doubts
I was wrong
I was assured
unafraid

At just 24. I knew more

No fear
I craved drama, challenge, stories to tell

Single-parenting
sounded powerful.

Her body

Ten years on:

Repeating
Unwitting single mum
Unplanned
Alone

I understood the words:

'Doing my best for one'

Certain
Assured
Need

I believe now

She knew more.

ROSEMARY

DAFFODILS MAKE ME CRY

Winter passed into spring
with little trouble this year. Did not
fight
to hold the frost in the ground.
Days grew like snowbells, slowly,
pushing up through the
earth
for a shining. Ringing.
I did a pregnancy test.

By mid-spring life had gone
and I ached, wished the days
weren't
getting longer.
We had daffodils
in the garden
that I hadn't planted
but my only child
loved.
She said, *Mummy, look*
at the trumpet
flowers, heralding
the spring,
except she didn't say
heralding
because she's only six.

I had never
thought of winter as life
or spring as death before I saw her
plucking those yellow petals
kneeling
on that damp soil
I knew
would stain her leggings.

There are only so many pairs
of leggings left to stain.

IN SEASON

Twelve months before my love fell into
someone else, we named her, Bow,
the shortened memory of her
conceived location. Our last holiday.

She would be just over a year
now, her eldest sibling not so sweet
sixteen, if plans were always fruitful
and darkened rooms with scanning machines
did not photograph the lack of life
inside of me. Removed with metal
like cattle prods, on the eve of our anniversary.

I never realised what it meant
for us: a future where I turned my back
on our family. Words could not
find the tongues between us,
only tears. Brick walls
that compensated for the growing distance
of our connection. Single cells mutated.
My belly empty with regret.

Veins coiled with medication
I couldn't stop; perforated foil rustling
in your head each time you tried
to touch me. I filled myself instead
with letters. When counting syllables
on my fingers, I remember Bow.

Counting one syllable – not Bow.

RIP HCG

I feel you leave
through my night skin
in a damp sheen, like I've been wrapped
in cling film for a week. And the dreams
have stopped; no more dissected puppies
or purple children with gaping holes
for faces, left in ballrooms
where I search
knee-deep through throat-slit blood
for something I know
has been forgotten.

My nipples can now be touched.
I can handle my emotions
and raw meat. I can empty
the food recycling bin without retching.
I can now stand
other people's morning breath.
I have the proof too:
a fading pinkish line, like something
left out in the sunlight
for a decade.

SELF-PORTRAIT IN A CONCAVE MIRROR

Today, to shrink is inside her nature.
She sits with pink sheer eyes
distant as the light that brought her
here. Cheeks glossed from hours of tears,

bones dressed in dissidence,
lips clipped in silence
like the night before the storm.
She knows there is no hope in this story.

Lost in the insignificance
of anything positive to say. The flush
of her six-week fragrance passes.

Summer is over.

I DIDN'T TELL THEM AT WORK

when I miscarried.
When I clutched my stomach
hunched in the loo
crying. I didn't tell them
how my body betrayed me,
felt grief dribble into my knickers.
I just gave myself a minute,
I cried, wiped, drew breath,
left the cubicle,
then drove myself home.

They still don't know.

A DIFFERENT TYPE OF BLOOD

When I bled the world began to turn backwards,
English words fell to Arabic scripture,
wallpaper grew roots and set forest fires,
nuclear fallout zones were cushioned and sofaed.
My womb gutted like the emptying of a colostomy bag
before it sent poison through me, and yet
it was the bleeding which was toxic. Not red.

Each month now, time splits and runs from me,
a river flow dictated by two disjointed moons.
Two futures, two directions, two movements,
but I am still. The blood smells old, like liver,
like a freshly mangled corpse from wild jaws.
I cannot help but smell it when I wipe, stare
at the brown/red streaks that reek of loss.

My soap is coconut
but I never get clean.
My blood type is O positive.

FOR MINE

The night you were taken
the dream was gone
of holding and protecting,
no spoken word to reflect
the darkness,

unravelling the mystery,
finding reasons,
complications, explanations.

Emptiness, loneliness,
lead in my belly fills the void,
weight on my chest suffocating,
struggling for breath.

Your life seeps through my veins,
your dreams flow from my tears.
Fond memories of aspirations.
Your hopes, your loves, my fears
lost in cotton wool balls and muslin sheets
soaked and mopped and doused,
weighed and dropped in plastic bags.
As you become nothing but
my last name and a number
and sent to labs for tests.

No one will see your face,
no one had felt your touch
or fallen in love with your smile.
You had not cried on your birthday
or laughed in the rain.
Made promises you could never keep,
picked daffodils in the spring.

COPING

You do not draw the curtains in the morning,
though I ask it of you almost every day.
Our room sits in the dark, with golden shadows
that fall on the walls where the sun wishes to play.
When I come home the room is as I left it,
brown, warm, lifeless, and neglected
as if our alarms have only just pierced the air,
as if we are just minutes from lying sleeping there.

Every afternoon,
I see this room
while you are still at work and I'm at home.
I see that you prefer to leave the day outside
to shelter in our duvet on your own.
I see that you and I are different,
my open windows
always lining this sanctuary.
Perhaps, my love,
perhaps too much.

You do not share your secrets in the evenings;
you prefer to keep them close and warm and brown.
I open mine up to the world.
The sun keeps shining.
Our bedroom is the place we lost them, true,
but also, my love,
the place where they were made.

I wish we had seen their faces.
I think they would have looked like you.

BLOOD RUN

I watch the blood run
afterwards, in the shower.
Clockwise circling, you both disappear.
You are not him, but better
in many ways. Though I wish
you spun in different directions.
I was a fool for thinking
I would find more.
I like the way you twist,
both of you.
Sometimes, I wish
we could all be one.

SURGEON'S BLUES

If you did not wear blue, what would it be?
In which shirt would we choose
to rest our trust?
Red: too true – right-felt tones of fear,
bright, fresh blood
drips.
Brown: mud, decomposing mulch,
hint of overcooked meat.
Green: full of spring –
new beginnings,
anticipation of fresh buds to appear.
Too clean
for white: angel's wings or paper napkins?
Filth sticks.
Black: not dead yet, though we tried.

Leave me here to lie
with your vast-sky hue
to dream of her
as I get high,
small scratch in the back
of my cold hand
limp.
Sharp prick – you laugh.
I fade.
You take her life and, with it,
mine.

RECURRENCY

I wanted to control my body
so I tied weights to my tongue
and put cushions on my ears.
I waxed my head
with a thousand red candles
like pulling impurities from
my scalp would cleanse the past.
In the mornings I injected helium
in my blood so I flew
and my toes blew up like plums
and when I wiggled them
they rubbed together, making
tiny squeaking sounds
like baby mice.

I wanted to control my body
so I restrained my heart
with spinach chains
and folic acid,
fluctuated between welcoming hope
and hating her.
I filled my house with jagged edges
to discourage a fall
and plugged my menstrual dam with
Cyclogest at twelve-hour intervals,
ate no peanuts,
no salami,
no brie.

But days grew cold,
blood circled in my universe
like the Milky Way
and I was forced to remember
how white tissues could burn red
at just a moment's notice.
I crossed my legs,

lay in my bed afraid to move,
cried tears that fell in familiar tracks
and prayed to a God I didn't believe in

again.

PICTURES

We'd seen that picture before,
littering our Facebook feed,
a sepia alien calling for grinning emoticons
bolstered with pages of congratulations.

We'd seen that picture before,
in friends' wallets and on their fridges,
pulled out for scrutiny and approval,
jokes about *Mummy's fingers, Daddy's head.*

We weren't offered a picture. Instead
they took us to a quiet room
where we could reflect
on that picture,
and that lack of sound.

PRET A MANGER

I met my friend for lunch last week.
After the muted fifteen years,
we still couldn't loosen the tongues
so tied, find any breath to share
or words to speak.
Death.
It builds up walls.

She watched my wriggling bump, the way
I could devour a chocolate pie, then with guilt
put two fingers down my throat.
The life that in ten weeks will be mine.
But hers is gone.
What's done is done.
Death.
The hurt and tears.

With folded arms across me
I tried to hide the nudging bones of knees
and elbows from her tired eyes
I forced a smile.
Her guilt strangled me.
Death.
She made that choice, not me.

SUPERSTITIONS

They said they didn't tell us
because they were superstitious, but we told them.
Weeks of sickness dragged through our friendship
like dumper trucks full of hidden accusations
and I asked, because my heightened senses
smelt it on them, but still they didn't say.
We told the world, wanted to tattoo it
on our stomachs and lift our clothes
to strangers on the street. I learnt to waddle.
Our scan dates were the same, but only they knew,
just told us later with a grimace, like admitting
they'd eaten the final sweet. We shared our
date like wedding cake, for all to share.

We went to different hospitals, the same
day. The secrets should have never mattered.
I would have forgotten
were it not for the pictures on the sonograph. Only
one heartbeat, one name.
They didn't tell us
'cause they were superstitious, but we told them.

SHE WOULD HAVE BEEN CALLED ROSE

The first time we made love after
they took her from me, I cried.
I pulled you into me and held on for dear
life. For indeed I knew then that life
was dear. Dear, dear life,
like a letter I would
never open.

I thought it would be gentle,
replacing those seeds,
but the pain split my insides like I
remembered my eighteen-year-old
self losing childhood.
My tears burnt.

There were no words; only glances
and motions like glue for our broken
spines, but we were not fixable.
Not then. My womb was dry, like barren,
fruitless prose.

The first time we made love after
they took her from me, I knew
that no other blooms would
fill her tome, her tomb.

I was not an apple pie virgin
full of bittersweet life.
I had been sucked dry.

You were not a conjunction
sticking us back together.

She was not to blossom.

STITCHES

Whilst attached to wires – drips in, drips out –
your tubes were tied. The sacrifice
for your own life, now every other cycle
halves your ten percent chance
to five. And no blue gown can tell you why.
No blue gown can justify why you're lying
in a clean, crisp recliner paralysed
from the painkillers
that barely touch the sides.

Tomorrow, the nurse, the officious one,
will come. Too quickly,
she will remove the catheter from your urethra,
wheel you to toilets, your bladder
under firm instruction
it must now perform on its own.
She'll add, in an over-zealous tone, that if you can
open your bowels, she'll sign the forms,
write up a prescription
and send you home.

Home. Home. Home.

Home to the mass
of cellophane-wrapped
supermarket flowers and Hallmark cards to order you
to 'Get Well Soon', a box that crackles
with co-codamol, wound-care instructions
and a dozen breeze-block sanitary pads.

Home, to two weeks free from employment
but a Netflix subscription
from the well-intentioned
husband
who doesn't know
what else he can do.

Home.
You'll decide you might lie, deny your poo,
beg for more morphine
and demand the bed
next to the window, away from the woman opposite
who seems incapable of comforting
her squalling new-born. You know, you hope
what she should do. You hope.

In seven days, you will return
for different blue gowns to check
on your healing, inspect the dissolvable stitches
intended to keep you
in one piece.

SUPPLEMENTS

The flowers sent for me, he received -
found pint glasses to turn into vases, cut
the stems under running water, like my
mother, on our wedding anniversary,
showed him to prolong their short and wilting life.
This time, in preparation for when I
could face the stairs

                 and linger between our
uncomfortable walls, damp with the stale
lilies neither of us wanted; to stain
our sideboards with the disintegrated
stamens I left untouched in fear I might
appear sliced with bitterness by cutting
prematurely. I left

             the blood-orange
dust to settle amongst the spine-creased
ante-natal books he never had a chance
to read. I told him not to answer
the door, said I deserved privacy and
space; everyone would know what I'd been through.
I needed

           clean sheets, sanitary pads,
arnica bath salts and vitamins:
A, B complexities, C, D and E
the vital minerals I left him to
Google-know-how and online shop for.
The list grew and grew. What was screen-clear
was his abhorrence to any further
reminders of dying.

         His life became reflected
in naked living room windows
of Sky sports, bottles of unopened
champagne, empty pizza boxes and too

many wilting petals. For him, there was
no hiding, even in the spare room.
Sometimes, I came down,

       to clutch my belly, show my pale face
and ask if it was not too much trouble
to put his shoes on to drive out for food.
I wore my dressing gown and forgot to wash
my hair. These norms were pointless,
I would say, when I couldn't even bear
to leave the house.

       Neighbours came most nights
with their left-over dinner wrapped
in silver foil on spare plates, like we had lost
everything. We gained more washing-up, pressure
for gratitude, wilting flowers with tiny hole-punched
cards of condolence. No-one thought to bring
artificial plants

       complete with vases – ones that never die.
Nor did they come to remove the stench
of stale waters, or stay to talk to him
about lighter stuff or ask him to join them for a beer.
And I never asked how much his shoulders
ached, with the burden of everyone
else's efforts.

RASPBERRY
LEAF

SPACE

She told me she cried when she heard,
sat on the step where she'd been standing
and sobbed stomach-bruising gulps that shook
her shoulders and tightened her gut.

She took my hand in hers and told me
that she cried when she heard, like me, like me.

Like me, the space in her grows daily, weeks
engraved like milestones, achievements, rewards.
We would have been sisters
looking forward
to the same spring, but now
my space echoes,
growing ever larger,
while hers kicks
and promises and lives.

My husband says we should be happy for
them, I know he's right, she cried for me,
but I can't help thinking of her swelling
belly – feeling those imaginary
movements
in my own, can't help cringing when
a pregnant
woman is given a seat,
or the last biscuit,
or extra smiles and care,
and sometimes
I wish we didn't reward them
for filling
their space, it is the emptiness
that hurts,
that deserves the last biscuit.

She took my hand in hers.
*It was probably
your hormones*, I said.

My weeks are holes,
chasms, gravestones,
while hers are
stepping stones towards a future.

MEASURING UP

She said his head measured
on the borderline centile of normal;
normal being an arbitrary spectrum
from *here to here*, she explained, her palms
facing about a metre from each other
but about a mile from us. We were told
not to worry too much. Not at this stage,
anyway. There was no point speculating,
Google searching, biting nails to the quick
or staring at the ceiling at 3am.

We just had to wait.

Another scan in a fortnight
would answer today's wordless debate.
Sent home with a referral to count Advent
in nightmares. To face a bleak Christmas break
and lightless New Year's Eve,
blank pages in the diary,
celebrations left to freeze. Holding on
to the premise he might just have a big brain –
abnormalities like this, that label *hydrocephalus*
when we had already chosen his name…

In bed with his picture, I examined
every line. Finding nothing
but shadows of imaginary faults. We decided
to postpone painting his room
but booked flights for the summer and avoided
one another. Because I did speculate as he browsed Google
and we both bit our nails at three in the morning.
We were trying to prepare for the
'worst-case scenario',
that by Easter we might be accepting
that we would still just be two.

WHAT THEY TELL YOU IS NOT TRUE

What they tell you is not true.
The woman who tells you
you're carrying low
so it's obviously a boy
does not have the power to
see through skin.
The man who tells you gold
will swing to or fro
does not actually know,
has no background in science.
You learn to never
in fact
learn.
In fact
you learn
tact – that surprising
thing
everyone forgets when they see
the protruding tummy button
and they say,
Childbirth really hurts.
Miriam's baby died.
They rip you apart.
It pulls at your heart,
what they say
stays with you,
weighs on you,
but it is not true, what they tell you.
Not true.

Life is just new –
each and every time.

PRAYING

There is a Catholic girl in me who comes when times are bad,
she prays and speaks to God and overrides my conscious.
I used to find her comforting, and sometimes God would
hear her in ways I'm not sure he ever heard me.
She is indoctrinated, making deals about my future,
her wishes and wants. She only comes when I am
desperate, weak. Promises God we will return to him,
but even I know God doesn't strike deals with Catholic girls
who can't come out to play anymore.
It doesn't work like that.

This time, I don't let her come, don't let her make deals
for my unborn children. She hovers, but I hesitate,
perhaps it's superstition, she didn't help before,
perhaps God knows she cannot really trade on my behalf.
I put pictures by the sides of my bed, Granny Deen,
Grannie Gillow, my husband's dear nan, matriarchs.
Stay back, Catholic girl. I ask the women of our line to bless
this new pregnancy. Give me strength, fill my womb.

The Catholic girl does not complain;
essentially we want the same thing.
We pray together,
don't make desperate deals.
The women of my line smile upon me.

REASSURANCE SCAN

You are not yet a baby, little bean,
but today I saw your heart beating
and you became real. I hope
your heart continues to beat,
that your centimetres double and grow
and thrive. I hope I do not drop
you, or let you down, as I did your brothers.

You are seven weeks old, little bean,
my womb the size of a lemon and yet
not bitter. A sickness sits in my stomach,
churns my fears and bile like cocktails
and I read every little message my body
sends between the lines on sticks, in constant
assessment. I am holding on to you.

One day, little bean, I hope to name you,
my rainbow child, I want to colour you
with all the battles Richard of York ever gained.
I hope to put my head on your chest and hear
your heart beating, as I saw it beat today,
as I listen to your sister's sometimes when she sleeps.
You are not yet a baby, little bean, but you are loved.

LITTLE BOY

I lie in bed and watch the ripples on my stomach reassure me of your life. Like a child's inflatable toy I am fluid, moving, jerking from left to right with no precision. I know you are a boy now and I wonder if you'll be like Daddy with his long back and dodgy knees, if he'll succeed in indoctrinating you into a world of football mania and sports watching. I grab my phone, start looking up feminist baby grows. We'll teach you to be balanced, and respectful, I think. Your sister will keep you straight.

There's a picture of Maya Angelou I was given one birthday past hanging in the hall. And still she rises. My feet are puffy and my tummy is dancing its own little polka, but I swing my hips to the side. You can kick as many footballs as you like, little boy, go to sleep with cricket bats as teddies. You can throw rugby balls like they're compliments, or pirouette your way through life, but you, my boy, my precious, longed-for, rippling boy, you will rise.

I am fluid with you, moving, dancing, swaying. There is a blank space on the wall in your bedroom. Your sister sees my mind. She helps me with the frame. We fill it. She is my warrior and you are my core – for now. Together we fill the space for you, until you are ready to fill it yourself.

BREATHING

and breathe
centred breath
in for four
and out
blow the waves around you
watch the ripples slowly flow
through the air
and breathe
centred breath
if he tries to tell me to breathe
I'll kill him
in for four
and out
blow his brains out
through the air
and scream
and breathe
and out
the midwife takes my hand
you're squeezing too tightly dear
you don't know your own strength
and breathe
and out.

BIG BOOTS

For you my mid-rift stretched
like I'd swallowed Army boots.
Breasts bloated
fingers swelled
I developed cankles.
My shoulders grew so broad
they could carry all the shoes
from all the pathways
of the world
for you. I stood
on the shoulders
of the women before:
Mary Ann
Patricia
Phyllis

and I grew tall enough
to never need heels
to see beyond (time)
I grew large enough
to cushion your limbs
wide enough to be
a battering ram
for your foes.

When you flooded from me
pain made me mighty
and fierce
but you split me
in half
made me great
and yet small again.
I looked at your face; crunkled, waxy, squashed
and I was just a tiny ant again, on the surface
of the world, terrified of big boots.

BABY BLUES

I'm terrified.
He's so little
I'm scared I'm going to break him.
I wake in the night to check his breath,
my hand on his chest,
mirror in front of his face.
I rouse him as I slip my hand in his baby grow
to check his temperature,
it is a mistake,
he screams.
I am reassured he is still alive.
I am mortified I woke him.
I want my mum.
I'm terrified.

FAMILY TIES

Your sister will visit, hold your hand
between the void of her purple plastic
chair and your blood pressure monitor.
Neither of you wants her to be here.
Your dad won't come. Not his place, he says,
to meddle in women's trouble, he would
only get under their feet. And your mother
still has her monthly migraine that started
last time she visited, last year. Your sister
will not let go of your hand, no letting go
of the clammy cling left from the residue
of the sticking plasters you peeled back
the edges from almost an entire lifetime ago.
You will wish then for a brother.

STEPFATHERS

You just became a dad, and I know you want to sit for hours and look at your son, wonder at his tininess and sweetness, smell his head, resist the urge to cover him in kisses. Last night you slept for no more than two hours.

There is a little girl in our room now. Excited about being a sister, well-rested away from the screams. She wants cuddles with the baby, cuddles with me. You gently tell her how special she is, how much you love her, how lucky her brother is that she exists. You pull on your clothes (I see the bleariness in your eyes), tickle her, hug her, cajole her into going swimming with you so 'Mummy can rest'. She giggles.

You just became a dad and I hear you on the phone saying it's the best thing you've ever done, yet you spend more time with my eldest than your newest. I go for a nap and I hear you teaching her how to hold her brother, how to carry him. I hear you tell her how much you love her, how much he does. You say we are a perfect family of four now.

You just became a dad biologically, but we both know you've been a dad for five years already. You are our hero. Thank you.

MRS SUPERMAN

I remember the day I confided
in my midwife and expelled a pond of tears
that drowned all available space
meant only for my newborn. She called the surgery
and spoke for me. They insisted I come in.

I took their prescriptions, colluded in their diagnoses
and kept it a secret from my husband. I engaged in an affair
with medication and wrapped the guilt like a natural
mother wraps her child. And when my best friend
lost her baby a month later, I couldn't cry.

I was the uncomfortable wife and mother whose misery
became a numbness I imagined was what I wanted: to feel
nothing. I was told not to breastfeed. That suited me. I needed
sleep. And misery was not on the agenda for the NCT weekly
meet. I told no one of the time I pushed the pram near the river

and tortured myself with the fantasy I could overturn
the weir. I had such power. No one warned me of the power.
I stopped taking the prescriptions, too ashamed to admit
to the superman I'd married that I couldn't handle
the precious burden he had given me.

THE FAIRY TALE

I have walked the miles
of ragged coastline
to find the journey
has no end – no answers
at the edges, no stone left

unturned. I choose in colours:
black, white, blue and red,
each so perfect in its
imperfection, it takes courage
to place them back. New life

grows from the undisturbed;
we find shells of ourselves
in which to hide. Sand
between my toes, I try
another viewpoint. The sun burns

down from the lowest point; I need
to discover another turning point.
I can't. Shadows become smaller,
tighter, darker from these feet split
from the journey beneath them. I stuff

my pockets with memories for tomorrow,
coral shades of corrugated edges, pebbles
to leave in Hansel and Gretel fashion
to show these shadows
their way back home.

THE CHANGING OF THE SPOTS

Your spots have changed, my dear,
said the leopard to his wife.
I have been watching you lie in the shade
and seen them cluster like ink blots.

There are patches now that are
missing, places I loved to run
my tongue across. Places I loved to feel
the unknown of the black beneath.

There are parts that were once
smooth yet now are patterned.
I see what was white has now become black
and black to red. In just a few

hours you have become another
cat. I would not recognise you
from the pack. Your spots have changed and you are
holding yourself in a different

way, as if your spots both bolstered
and softened you. As if your spots
both made and unmade you. I have watched you
lie in the shade and before my eyes

you have gone all Rorschach.
Your spots have changed, my dear,
said the leopard to his wife. Yes, she replied.
Hold your child, he's but a minute old.

YES I DO

Firstly let me start by saying,

I love you.

Today I wash dishes
change 3 pooey nappies and 2 wees, the ones she did,
not me. No time
for my own release
changed clothes twice, his and mine
(still in my maternity clothes 4 months on
by the way) Have you noticed?
had my nipples yanked
in every inconceivable direction
whilst the surrounding area,
what's it called?
Memory
        It seems to be... as inconsistent
As my use of tenses, punctuation and generally my ability
to offer anything but

Breasts. That's what I was recalling; swell like balloons
about to pop
and all on less than 3 hours sleep. Can you understand that
correlation?
How was the spare room for you last night, dear?
I imagine quiet.

I took the other child to school
with food for lunch. Did I have lunch? dunno. I know I ate half
a packet of hobnobs at some point. Or was that yesterday?
When was yesterday, the last breath of sunlight
a clean PE kit
her homework
and a white sheet for Greek day
(that didn't have any stains on it
by the way) I'm still talking about our other child, the one who
definitely

had lunch and got picked up
by me
and I hadn't had time for a wee.
I know I mentioned that earlier but
It's a thing
so I wet myself when I sneezed
at the school gate
and yes, I haven't washed for a week.
Have you noticed?
How was your shower this morning dear?
I imagine lovely

Ah yes, I did eat, I remember

The over ripe banana
a triangle of brie –
the big ones – I bit it off like a sandwich
the end of a carrot
the end of a bowl of porridge
(I spilt that on the baby but it was cold
so you don't need to worry)
half an apple
3 Boosts
because I was only going to buy a twin pack
but they were on buy-2-get-1-free
I'm trying to be thrifty now – more hungry mouths.
and cold macaroni cheese.
It looked nice when you ate it warm,
Was it?

I drank
several glasses of water
including one I think
that had stewed on the bedside table for a few days
but in my breast-feeding
craze filled thirst
I didn't care.
Can you get salmonella from water?
How was your after work beer?

I imagine refreshing.
May I just reiterate that I love you.

I spent a lot of the day
I Think it was day, raining.
sat
staring at the mess
letting the baby lick my nipples raw
and sleep
upon my chest. Her not me
though I tried
to keep my eyes open
I know it's dangerous to snooze.
I had about 2 hours hands free
When I carried all 15 pounds of him
in the sling
so I could unload the top of the dishwasher
and do those things you can only do
without bending over:
cleaning sides, kitchen ones
worktops.
and sweeping
and food shopping. That might not sound like much
to achieve in the two hours
that felt more like like 5.

I hear the envy in your voice
when you phone from work and I tell you
he smiled today.
You are right to be envious.
It made my heart sing.
I want to think of less cliché terms
but I am tired
and the memory thing -
I've lost words. Lost words that always felt like mine.

I remember some –
the precious ones –
I love you

I say them every day.
I love you
but no – you can not go on another Stag do
and no – you can not go and watch the football
and no – don't spend our precious money on Warhammer
bugs
and no – I won't have time to turn on that incredibly
dangerous iron and iron your bloody shirts
and no – I don't need your mother to come and stay for a
week
and yes – he is a gorgeous boy
and yes – she is a perfect big sister
and yes – I do have the better job
and yes – if only he'd take a bottle
and yes – I do want you to take him for a drive
and yes – I am a nag
and yes – I do, I do, I do

I do love you.

THE MACHINE

Twenty-five thousand metres
rowed every seven days;
one hundred and eighty thousand,
three hundred and thirty-three
double-pulls each lunar cycle,
going nowhere
but the bathroom scales
and the next belt loop down
a size. Nine months to pile
twelve kilos around my middle,
twenty-four hours to drop six,
fifty percent left for me
to deal with whilst you thrive.

Burn a single calorie per five metres.
My final push left me
with your deficit,
one pull, an inhale-exhale
exchange for two millimetres squared
of Kit Kat or ice cream.
Breastfeed the quarter of every year.
Wait. Weigh it up. Row.
Row. Row. Row
my bloat.

Don't eat to appetite. Tuck
spare tyres into support wear.
Go to the kitchen to avoid
mirrors or to the inside
of Nike Air Max to take
my mind outside. Only dream
of Malbec, white carbohydrate
and cheese.
Row. Don't breathe.

THREE IN A BED

I created lives to somehow save me. Cover cracks with Band-Aids. Complete me or hide me behind Mother Nature's swollen tummy, leaking breasts, stretch marks, bio oil, nosebleeds, kilos of Quality Street. Bleeding gums, scans, due dates. Kits to predict ovulation, menstruation and, at last, a viable conception. Morning sickness embraced – those mornings missed – escaping into panic of impending miscarriage.

More tests, more tests, more tests at sixteen weeks. One in ten thousand risk of one syndrome... or another. At thirty-six it rises, to one in two hundred and fifty. That sounds high. The maths, of course, doesn't apply as in your mind, the risk's been made. What number would blind you? And what would you do, anyway? What ratio to decide to destroy? One in one hundred? Fifty-fifty? As by now you're in: belly slightly bulging, faint internal flutterings.

There's a photo and you keep it by your bedside. Not in direct sunlight as that would fade it. And every day you check it still has arms and legs, a spine, toes and fingers it sucks from time to time. One disproportionate head. Four beating chambers: counted, measured, squared. A liver, two kidneys, a healthy placenta – the other end of which attaches to every sense of inside. So you decide no decisions will ever be made. Let fate deal her hand; destiny will be the only controller of this game.

Assigned a midwife. She becomes your mother in another life. You open up like you've been shut forever and she seems to like it. One week she's absent, on some holiday or annual leave. You feel abandoned, rejected, frustrated to explain yourself to someone else. Like exploring the flirtations of another lover.

Birth plans: you write yours to appease your sense you're in control. Soon to discover they're not worth the paper they're written on. When does nature not come undone? Your plan was never to be at home, lowing like farmyard cattle to please no one but the yoga-breathing antenatal crowd. You wanted drugs, preferably before the labour started, sterile walls and monitors to check your baby's heartbeat. You got none. The plan unravelled. The rest's too nasty to remember. The mind does that, otherwise you would never have another.

Newborns fuck you up. Not that anyone bothered to tell you that. Well, not until you were up the duff. It's a secret club you can't be a member of until it's too damn late. When the breasts have sagged, the nipples bleed and you can't stop eating your own body weight in Maltesers just to constantly feed the limpet who may as well still be inside for all the space you get – but need. You're so dog tired, you fall asleep whilst changing his nappy, on your knees with the little fucker still attached, milking you for every ounce you've got. It's that – or be tortured with the screams.

The screams. The screams...

There comes a time when you realise. This has to stop. You can't keep sharing your body and your bed. Three's a crowd, husband's getting tense. It's been six months. Enough is enough. Time to control cry the little blighter in his cot. That shit's not for the fainthearted. But we won't go into that – and never mind the stretch marks, iron deficiency, leaky bladder and saggy fanny... that screaming in his cot at night...
That trauma would be enough
to put you off. For life.

INSIDE OUT

I miss the flutter of you
beneath my skin. Not the frantic
grip of fingernails across
busy roads. I miss the turn
of your anticipated spine against
my own. Not the whine when
the hairbrush struggles through
your unkempt hair. I miss the tease
of toes, knees, elbows on my pelvis,
the stretch of limbs that catch
my ribcage. Not the complaints
my thought-out dinner isn't to your taste.
I miss the dream, the secret kept to myself,
not to feel the tide of you retreat
with the triggers of the moon.
I only miss this now I realise
you were the final one.

RIOJA

BIRTH STORY

I would write the story of your life,
condense significant moments into bullet points
like when you started walking
or your first lessons
or those times I looked at you and wondered if I'd ever really
love you
past that bleak post-birth depression.

I would write that I read the books
and walled myself in ruled paper and natural parenting tips
and that when they talked about instincts
I felt sick
and when they talked about love I felt numb
and that I waited nine and a half months and twenty-seven
years to be a mum
but never felt that motherhood had come.

If I chunked your moments down
I'd know the dates of all your firsts,
your smiles and foods and kisses and words,
and I'd be able to chronicle when babyhood ended
and you became a girl,
but timelines of your brilliance
wouldn't tell of our experience,
wouldn't lift Pandora's lid and admit
that though I kept your records
I secretly felt unfit.

I should write that I cried,
afraid of the question marks that hung from your nappies,
afraid to say I couldn't feel –
that would make it real.
I should write that I breastfed
because the midwife said
I should
and I was lucky I could.

If I were to write the story of your life I'd say
I told the world I loved you
and that no one knew
how scared I was that I didn't.
I would write how amazing you are
that you survive
me as your mum.

I would write our story
about you, my beautiful first,
if I thought it would help others cope.
But maybe I just need to write your name,
my girl, my Hope.

Because now I know you, dear daughter,
I carry you in my core
and you run through my blood like helium
lifting my feet from the floor.
I should write that even when I think life is stuffed
things adjust.
That babies are hard
and so is love.

I would write the story of your life
but it would never do you justice.

BREASTFEEDING

It's the middle of the night.
All is calm.
Outside a street light glows orange,
illuminating the people carriers and Volvos.

Suddenly I wake,
pulled from my dreams,
vanishing memories of my pre-pregnancy body
yanked out with her screams.
The charm breaks and my breasts burst;
I am awash with milky glue.
She carries on screaming,
angry with thirst.

They ache,
these mammouth Jordan-esque melons that throb and pulse
and stretch to fill,
and though the rivers run into puddles on my pillow
the oceans rage in my mammary glands still.

So I rise to her cries and sleepily stomp to her room.
How can he sleep through?
And as I knock my head on her mobile
and my grandfather's clock chimes three
I reach over the cot to my daughter.
She stops her screams, sees me and smiles.

And through all the sleepless nights, the body cavities and
pain,
with that smile all is forgiven – until she wakes me up again.

SASHA

If I eat three Weight Watchers Mars bars,
does that count as a binge session?
And when David comes home from
not quite working and complains because
I hung his saggy elastic boxer shorts up
outside the flat where our only neighbour
could see them but the air could make them
smell so fresh, do I ask him about the
cauliflower and garlic he forgot to buy?
Do I moan that I am the fabric of this sari
we are woven up in and yet I have lost
my beginnings, and my end? Should I?
I open the fridge and see that the CIA
bugged my parmesan due to the fact
it has been so long sitting there it is not at risk
of escape. I knew there was a buzzing
on my phone line but thought it was the flies
around the nappies David refuses to touch.
He says the korma stains deter him and he
has such sensitive skin. The baby doesn't
cry anymore, not since prohibition and
that man who masturbates in our cellar.
I pinched him the other day to check
that he was real and he laughed.

THE OXYMALLEON

There's an Oxymalleon stirring on the edge of my sleep,
jumping through the air like a yoyo.
He's gallant as folktales, heavy as lust,
like a deeply insistent Quasimodo.

Let me in past your debris, in past your locks,
let me slither and wither and wilt.
Won't you breathe me and taste me and swallow me whole
and stop smothering me with your guilt?

He lurks, like a memory, on the edges of my womb,
though I'm not much inclined to acknowledge him.
He pushes hard on my chest, says it's a kiss from the best,
calls it tongue-squibbling Oxymalleon frolicking.

Let me in past your barriers, your oversized carriers.
Let me eat you all up for my tea.
For I am a starving Oxymalleon, poor Oxymalleon I am.
Only your sweat, blood and tears will appease.

And in the corners of my nightmares, the roof of my dreams,
under the very crotch of my stall,
there lurks my Oxymalleon, my free Oxymalleon,
to keep me from sleeping at all.

SCRIPTURE

She lets the Jehovah's witnesses sit
on her sofa and drink her tea while she
changes the baby's nappy and butters toast
for the two-year-old. She tries to read the
scripture they give her with one hand, whilst
jigging the baby on her hip. She drapes
a muslin on her shoulder to hide the
leakage of her breasts. Matthew 28:
19: the world is a shocking place to
be, we must be baptised, we must have faith.
The baby's teething biscuit drops in a
soggy gunge mess on the floor. The other
child runs a toy car up her legs. She smiles.

My husband left me, she says simply. *Just
got up one day, walked out of the door.*
The woman witness shifts in her seat.
Perhaps we should go. It's not a good time.
They hand their empty tea cups back. Thanks.
She sees them out, closes the door. *All gone,*
the toddler says.
Yes, she thinks, like Daddy.

THE LAST SUPPER

Some company would be good –
you need not even speak
or listen to the nothingness
I have to say. Just be.
I write this as I sit,
at an empty table where seven faces
left to say goodnight.
Whilst I fought tears, leant into them
and singed my unwashed hair
on the candle that remained bright
just seconds after they had left.
I am sorry.
Everyone looked tired;
I know I could make them well…
Lack of altruism disallows me that.
Forgive me.
Let the lines upon your faces
not run too deep and the sadness
that beseeches you be lost
through moonlit nights
of unbroken sleep.
I would take it from you,
every prick of it, if I could.
Perhaps I am already –
by sitting in an empty restaurant,
half-cut and weeping
across this scrawling page.
Yet despite my self-indulgent words,
I know it does not make your pain less.

UPCYCLING?

The last one's gone, discarded last week
with the Christmas wrapping paper,
Prosecco and Amazon boxes.
There is now the air of New Year glitz.

The kids hate her, say she never speaks
directly to them with her painted Essex lips
but flashes her expensive teeth at Daddy
and makes him blush. Too much.
I don't remember ever making him blush.

She wears white jeans, even on grey days,
wraps hope with sequins, cashmere and diamante studs.
She clicks efficiently in kitten heels,
has makeovers, spa membership, Botox,
and knows what dinner lighting
will effectively backdrop her clothes.

I want to lose weight. More weight.
I want to paint myself in pheromones,
hang glass pendants from my neck, effortlessly,
and work the backless bra to enhance
whatever chance is left of his desire.
I want to charm my bracelet
heavy with other men's money.

I want to remember everyone's birthday
and never leave my lover hungry
on Valentine's. I might buy an Epilady
or suffer a Brazilian monthly. I might
apply for a Debenhams card and an overdraft.
I might get a job in PR and start blow-drying
my highlighted hair. And I am definitely
going to learn to roll sushi.

The kids hate her. My daughter says
she is not impressed by the way she hangs
off Daddy and gets in the way
of their bedtime stories. But still she comes
with nothing more or less
than that.

THE BURN

Pressure builds in a consciousness
full of words. Desire to break free
and make crazy love burns holes
in the madness as we dream.

I share my bed with a princess;
light breath whispers through reality.
She wriggles in her sleep. Unconditionally,
she loves me, this girl who will soon wake
and whirl with the energy of a sun-drenched
fairground ride – before she leaves.

Empty rooms again. Words only have
this page to be heard. There is a dead time
to it, in which I breathe the scent
of her pale skin. The child who gives this house
its home. Once she is gone, the poem is written.
The desire to break free, gone. No more crazy
holes burned in the family that once
made us one.

LIKE MOTHER, LIKE DAUGHTER

She's ten. The same age I was when my
mother made me watch the release that day,
on the black and white portable my father
bought from Oxfam. When my mother told me
I should remember exactly where I was
that day, she said I would be grateful. I was
ten, as my daughter is now. His name meant
only oranges and grapes and Cape Town.

I am a mother now, and I remember
that grainy set, that grainy day, when my
mother, Gran, forced me to watch a tiny
black man cry. My mouth was full of facts
and protests, but I know where I was then,
when I was ten. I remember. I tell
my daughter where I was, and take her to
Occupy. She is ten. Never too young.

She's ten. The same age I was when I
learnt the name Mandela, when I thought I
understood equality, but in truth
knew only home. She recycles, knows not
to buy Nestlé, comes with me to polls.
She cried the morning we voted Brexit,
writes bad words in her diary about Trump.
She is ten. She thinks more than you could know.

CO-DEPENDENT

for Evelyn

She looks at me with her big eyes, her questions, words,
ideas beyond her understanding, and I look back at her,

my eyes tired with sadness and wonder and the realisation
that the magnitude of her inquisitive mind

may take her far in life. I hope the weakness of the woman
I am will not repeat itself. I plough through the demands:

fun and food, but only able to offer muted versions,
both barely touching her sides.

I request a sufficient amount of love and affection
to ensure my cup is always half-full.

I feed her stomach and she feeds my soul,
this bottomless pit that can never have too much.

With her impossible energy, she manages to catch me
and in her own way, she saves me every day.2017

Remember us as kids, being told about spiders –
how in our sleep, they crawled across our faces,
laying their eggs in our ears? Or was it our mouths,
and we would eat them?
Either way, it freaked me out.
And how, if you looked in the mirror
at exactly midnight, Satan would stand behind
trying to stuff his cock in
(though I have a suspicion this may have just been me)?

No. Of course not. I forget, sometimes,
you are not me.

And in your world, even twenty years

from now, your definition will be something else:
perhaps that your mother left your father
for a fanatical Buddhist. And if that wasn't bad enough,
she fucked your teacher – and not quietly.
No. She was loud. About everything.
Even those piercings screamed
of the middle-class breakdown, just days before Christmas –
like she couldn't have waited, like everything
had to be linked to her meltdown. Her preoccupation with
being the queen of clichés. Even to the anniversary of
her own mother's leaving, so she could write out
the performance of a lifetime.

But she forgets, as you do, that she is just human.
She forgets that sometimes, often, usually, always,
she is supposed to put you first.
She forgets you are just fifteen, with an insecurity as blistering
as the youth group summers blazoned on her skin
without sunscreen: white skin, acne, a designer hoodie
hiding the private dental braces and haircut salvaged
with Daddy's Brylcreem.

I'm so sorry, son. So sorry to leave you flailing
amongst the tides that threaten
to take you under. I never told you
I have the lifeboat, that pop-up magic trick
to take you places you've not yet dreamt to go to…
Because you don't know. Not yet.

You're barely ready to take the rudder.
You have so many mistakes
we have to watch you go through.
Though I can barely breathe and witness the monstrosity of life
fuck you up, your young life struck
in its beginning by the first whiff of definition:
screwed up, spoiled, opportunities galore
for you only to decide to stick two fingers up
at every institution. You have no realisation of your heritage,

cattle-grazing grandparents' class struggle
('cause that ain't cool)
and then your grandmother's Thatcher dilemma
of the council house that I called home
and the subsequent Blair meritocracy
where they all wore post-modern jumpsuits, shoulder pads
to protect what everyone knew as feminist rights
and journeyed through with whiskey chasers,
Benson & Hedges and Dire Straits.
Seemingly just to get you here.

But why would you? You are fifteen.
You are Snapchat, streaks, Facebook likes –
you are living in your moment of designer-clad,
white-powder-snorting, Instagram-liking,
epiphany of man-made fibre popularity.
But I cannot deny that you are nothing more,
or less, than a product of your genes.
We are all the same street corner, simply reunited.
Polyester-zipped generations of the nineties.
It does not matter.
You say *sick*. I was sick. I am sick.
But tomorrow, we might all be sweet.
Saccharine-sweet mixers of the street.
When I was pregnant, you were no more real
or present or accountable than the shapeshifting,
raised-temperature, oestrogen-producing, progesterone-
defending
macabre of the dream-world. You never asked to be here.
You were just two pink lines.
You were new bud growth
from this old tree.

THE SHOULDER SONG

I sense her body, limbs half my size,
just an arm-stretch next to me.
Her skin breathes
in the light-polluted city-dark.
I know she is awake.

I want to scoop her,
rescue the single shoulder
from the gaping mouth
of the duvet and lay her hair
beside mine in cascades
of yesterday. But I don't.

ROUGH AND TUMBLE

I saw you push him today
and secretly I applauded you
whilst reprimanding.
For two years he's been
asking you to do it.
You look at me,
steady,
say *sorry* quickly,
for you knew that it was coming,
and you give the required apology
hugs and kisses
to us both.

Three minutes later when
my back is turned
you push him again.
I hear him fall.
I think of all the bruises
you haven't yet had the language to explain.
I continue chopping the carrots
for you both
to share.

ELEVENSES

She looks too pretty
lying back on the sofa
rubbing her eyes
hugging her monkey.

I put her hair in bunches
knowing she will wait
to rub the back of her head
into a bird's nest for me

to tease out later.

COMFORT BLANKET

I find her
stash of me: dirty laundry
stuffed between her
freshly-made sheets. My favourite jumper, lost
last Wednesday, summer's dressing-gown
and last week's nightdress – the washing
labels curled like cigarette papers,
ribbed with fingernail dirt
and rubbed against her
top lip. Teddy's limbs splayed,
rejected at the skirting board.
Its glass eyes pressed
into corners
of the toy-box.

BEDTIME

Last night we came home late
and went straight to bed.
You said you didn't want a story.
I tucked you in,
gave you a big kiss and cuddle,
then lingered a moment more in the half-light
to admire your velvet skin.
You opened one eye
lazily.
Mummy, you said bedtime now.
Go away.

FIRST DATE

When the girl saw the boy
for the very first time,
he scaled the bricks of the park wall.
Scabbed flesh poked at her
through rips in his regulation trousers.

He had mud on his face
in a perfect statement
like he had meant to smudge it
just the way Tarzan would.
She thought she might lie; change her name.

When the boy saw the girl
for the very first time,
she straddled a baby swing,
wet wisps stuck at one cheek,
free of the claws that pinned down her fringe.

She had a hole in her tights
that showed her grey-white knickers
when a whistle of spring wind blew.
She must have known it was there.
Perhaps she hoped he would see it.

When they both saw each other
for the very first time,
they scrabbled in boxes of penny chews.
Both snatched at the Black Jacks,
the winner taking the last one first.

THE SONG

after Ed Sheeran

Do you know what this song is about?
he asks. Can you imagine that,
to see your dad slowly to forget
and then to die,
not knowing how much
he was loved? I nod, tears in my eyes.
How did this boy become
so wise? I feel for him.
Just into double figures,
he senses everything. I know,
only too well, the curse
such sensitivity brings.
Am I equipped to deal
appropriately with his offerings:
so many questions? With a mind of
the many-lived, physically in the mirror image
of his daddy?
So much easier living knowing nothing.
To be a child of simplicity where life
glides without incident.

MOTHER'S WORK

I smell his trousers and they smell
of dog and cat and half-sucked lollipops.

But it is just his Scooby-Doo pants I chuck
at the washing machine's gaping mouth,

hungry for familiar patterns.
The cling film's end recoils from remnants of supper,

as the dishwasher spits,
swallows memories in one.

There is no bark, no cry of feline
expectation in this house; only their sweet wrappers

stuck inside unemptied pockets and bottoms of socks
still mismatched from organised drawers

at Daddy's. I mop sadness from each tear duct,
all attempts to drown the ties between us coursing

through my veins. I peg us out in equal measure:
a spoonful of detergent, a sliver of Sunday's breast.

I smell his trousers. They smell
of another woman's home.

2017

Remember us as kids, being told about spiders –
how in our sleep, they crawled across our faces,
laying their eggs in our ears? Or was it our mouths,
and we would eat them?
Either way, it freaked me out.
And how, if you looked in the mirror
at exactly midnight, Satan would stand behind
trying to stuff his cock in
(though I have a suspicion this may have just been me)?

No. Of course not. I forget, sometimes,
you are not me.

And in your world, even twenty years
from now, your definition will be something else:
perhaps that your mother left your father
for a fanatical Buddhist. And if that wasn't bad enough,
she fucked your teacher – and not quietly.
No. She was loud. About everything.
Even those piercings screamed
of the middle-class breakdown, just days before Christmas –
like she couldn't have waited, like everything
had to be linked to her meltdown. Her preoccupation with
being the queen of clichés. Even to the anniversary of
her own mother's leaving, so she could write out
the performance of a lifetime.

But she forgets, as you do, that she is just human.
She forgets that sometimes, often, usually, always,
she is supposed to put you first.
She forgets you are just fifteen, with an insecurity as blistering
as the youth group summers blazoned on her skin
without sunscreen: white skin, acne, a designer hoodie
hiding the private dental braces and haircut salvaged
with Daddy's Brylcreem.

I'm so sorry, son. So sorry to leave you flailing

amongst the tides that threaten
to take you under. I never told you
I have the lifeboat, that pop-up magic trick
to take you places you've not yet dreamt to go to…
Because you don't know. Not yet.

You're barely ready to take the rudder.
You have so many mistakes
we have to watch you go through.
Though I can barely breathe and witness the monstrosity of life
fuck you up, your young life struck
in its beginning by the first whiff of definition:
screwed up, spoiled, opportunities galore
for you only to decide to stick two fingers up
at every institution. You have no realisation of your heritage,
cattle-grazing grandparents' class struggle
('cause that ain't cool)
and then your grandmother's Thatcher dilemma
of the council house that I called home
and the subsequent Blair meritocracy
where they all wore post-modern jumpsuits, shoulder pads
to protect what everyone knew as feminist rights
and journeyed through with whiskey chasers,
Benson & Hedges and Dire Straits.
Seemingly just to get you here.

But why would you? You are fifteen.
You are Snapchat, streaks, Facebook likes –
you are living in your moment of designer-clad,
white-powder-snorting, Instagram-liking,
epiphany of man-made fibre popularity.
But I cannot deny that you are nothing more,
or less, than a product of your genes.
We are all the same street corner, simply reunited.
Polyester-zipped generations of the nineties.
It does not matter.
You say *sick*. I was sick. I am sick.
But tomorrow, we might all be sweet.
Saccharine-sweet mixers of the street.

When I was pregnant, you were no more real
or present or accountable than the shapeshifting,
raised-temperature, oestrogen-producing, progesterone-
defending
macabre of the dream-world. You never asked to be here.
You were just two pink lines.
You were new bud growth
from this old tree.

NUMBERS GAME

Husband vacuums rotten food
from the shelves in the fridge.

Son number one 'Jailbreaks'
an iPhone, refurbished and recycled
between new mates. He has a branded
status symbol to maintain.

Number two has fucked off
into town, chinos stuffed with the profits
from selling knock-off cans of Coke
to his mates in the playground.

Number three, seemingly, can't stop
his arms from flailing as he imaginary cricket bowls
incessantly in 'that way', MumsNet claims,
all ten-year-old boys will do.

Number four, foot fresh out of plaster,
seems intent on breaking another bone,
somersaulting – badly – from chair to sofa,
sofa onto floor.

We think we might ring
a specialist helpline for number five.
There must be some syndrome or label
to attach this little fucker back together.

Number Six slams doors
with the ferocity of the predestined
teenage bitch who will inevitably
despise even the fact I'm still alive

The vacuum ceases to function,
blocked by a more mature piece of cheese.

White noise fills me.

ACKNOWLEDGEMENTS

Hannah:

I must address my eternal awe of the power of the reproductive system, without which, I would never have had the privilege to write around a subject so rich with emotion. And so to Thommie, the perfectly challenging and fearless collaborator in the production of this collection – thank you.

Few words can address my gratitude to my six incredible children, and the four tiny buds that never found their own life. It is true to say that at twenty-five years old, I had no idea what I was signing up for and that after eighteen years of motherhood, I still feel pretty clueless. I will never forget the support of the wonderful staff of the NHS, particularly Jenny at Pulteney Practice, true friends and unique support networks that helped to scaffold the intricate web of my unique experience of early Motherhood.

And to Lee, who against all odds, remains at my side and helps nurture me into the mother I always hope I can be –Salut!

Thommie:

When I started writing this poetry it was as a form of healing and never meant for public consumption, but through the love and strength of the amazing women I have around me and, of course, through Hannah's bravery and encouragement it has become something I am proud to share in all its bloody glory.

I must thank the NHS; the staff at Southmead Hospital's early pregnancy unit, the midwives at Weston Ashcombe Birth Centre, all of whom are outstanding in their professionalism and sensitivity; Deb, my midwife, and my consultant Emma, who supported me throughout my recent pregnancy.

Being a woman is an absolute privilege and pleasure, but I would not be able to write the way I do without the support of *some amazing men in my life. My husband is a constant rock and forgives me for plastering our lives over pages, my brother is the best uncle to my children and support to us all, and now I have a little boy, who will grow to continue this pattern of great men and always remind me that I am one of the lucky mums, one of the lucky women.*

Joint thanks:

Both of us must thank Clive Birnie, Bridget Hart and the Burning Eye team for believing in us and their untiring work in promoting artists.

We must also thank Tim Cox for his inspirational artwork on the cover and for each section of this book. He listened to our ideas and concepts and then blew us away with his incredible design. It is fair to say that his vision far surpassed our own and we are forever grateful.

Lightning Source UK Ltd.
Milton Keynes UK
UKHW01f2335300818
328057UK00002B/46/P

9 781911 570271